Tuchy's Law And Other Contrarian Quotes To Help You In Life's Journey

Tuchy's Law And Other Contrarian Quotes To Help You In Life's Journey

Tuchy Palmieri

2007

Tuchy's Law And Other Contrarian Quotes To Help You In Life's Journey

Dedication: To all the wonderful people who crossed my path and gave me thought provoking words to live or not live by. To Justin Sterling, Werner Erhard, Scott Peck, Leo Buscaglia, Wayne Dyer, Anthony Robbins, Deborah Tannen, Florence Scovill Shinn, Abigail Trafford, and all the great men and women helping others to be all they could be. And to my men's team for their unwavering support through the last 22 years, to John Moser, one of my oldest friends, whose countless hours advising and editing made my books happen. And finally to my precious wife Susan, who sends me off each day with great words and greets me with kind and loving words when I return.

TUCHY'S LAW AND OTHER CONTRARIAN QUOTES TO HELP YOU IN LIFE'S JOURNEY

1)   He who laughs, lasts.

2)   Turn your stumbling blocks into stepping-stones.

3)   Trifles make perfection, but perfection is no trifle.
      -Michelangelo

4)   Our grand business in life is not to see what lies dimly at a distance, but to do what lies clearly at hand.

5)   We are not creatures of circumstance; we are creators of circumstance.

6)   Don't tell me how the watch works; tell me what time it is.

7)   If you always tell the truth you don't have to remember what you said.

8)   You know you're old when you've lost all your marbles.

9)   You cannot have an opinion about something if you know nothing about it.
      —John Zaleski

10)   Knowledge quiets anger. Wisdom overcomes fear.

11) The reasonable man adapts himself to the conditions that surround him. The unreasonable man adapts surrounding conditions to himself. All progress depends on the unreasonable man.
—*George Bernard Shaw*

12) Because of deep love, one is courageous.
—*Lao Tse*

13) Diplomacy: the art of jumping into troubled water without making a splash.
—*Art Linkletter*

14) Nothing can bring you peace but yourself.
—*Ralph Waldo Emerson*

15) Self-trust is the first secret of success.
—*Ralph Waldo Emerson*

16) All good things come to he who waits, provided he knows what he's waiting for.
—*Woodrow Wilson*

17) Adversity causes some men to break and others to break records.

18) Friendship is like a bank account. You can't keep drawing on it without making a deposit.

19) Of all the things you wear, your expression is the most important.

20) It is through confusion that you finally come to clarity.

21)   To know the road ahead, ask those coming back.
—*Chinese proverb*

22)   Arms are for hugging.

23)   Know yourself, win half your battles; know your
enemy, win half your battles. Know yourself and
your enemies, win all your battles.
—*Sun Tzu, Art of War. 600 B.C.*

24)   Most people only hear themselves talk.
—*John Zaleski*

25)   If you are losing a tug-of-war with a tiger, give him
the rope before he gets to your arm. You can always
buy a new rope.

26)   You need a plan to follow the plan.
-*Walt Capone*

27)   Angels are not privy to plots hatched in hell.

28)   God gives the nuts but he does not crack them.

29)   We make a living by what we get but we make a life
by what we give.

30)   It is not the sun nor the lack of water that makes a
desert barren but the absence of faith.
-*Linda Mullin*

31)   There is a light from which we are all born, all fed,
forever nursed; a life we know as home, a light we
know as God.
-*Brett*

32) It is easier to clean things up as they pop up rather than as they pile up.
    -Don Hanson

33) Selfishness is not living as one wishes to live; it is asking others to live as one wishes to live.

34) My hunger is not for food.

35) Anything maintained by force is doomed to fail.
    —*Henry Miller*

36) The proof of my decisions will show up today in my actions.

37) Anything that is motivated by fear will be temporary.

38) People will expend more energy to reduce their pain than they will to induce their pleasures.

39) The oxen are slow but the earth is patient.

40) It's important to do the important things that have importance.

41) Important things are important only when they are important.

42) Success is getting up just one more time than you fall down.

43) Wisdom comes more from living than from studying.

44) Don't be afraid to go out on a limb. That's where the fruit is.

45) Truth is shorter than fiction.
-Flo O'Brien

46) The only ones who really strike out in life are the ones who don't play.

47) Locks only keep honest people honest.
—Judy Rudnick

48) If you don't make dust you will eat dust.

49) Sometimes when you look the least you find the most.
—Paul O'Brien

50) Growing old isn't for the weak.

51) Never lose your sense of humor.
—Tammie Burns

52) A little house well filled, a little land well tilled, and a little wife well willed, are great riches.

53) He that falls in love with himself has no rival.
—Benjamin Franklin

54) Every man is the architect of his own fortune.
—English proverb

55) Everything has its season.

56)   Know where the boss is at all times.
        -Lou Aquavia

57)   Stupidity has no limit.
        —Vladimir Slep

58)   Not always but often, no news is bad news.

59)   Some truths are personal in nature. In such cases
        it is quite possible to have conflicting and contrary
        things be true.

60)   Wisdom is a matter of knowing how much is
        enough.

61)   "Enough" is a matter of knowing how much is
        enough.
        -Arlene

62)   One man's work is another man's play.

63)   Sex is like basketball; the last minute is very
        exciting.
        -Yolanda Chevez

64)   You can't change, unless it's for a dollar bill.
        -Karen Mileski

65)   A hammer shatters glass but forges steel.

66)   Whether you choose to paddle down the river,
        walk the pathway, ride the highway, or climb the
        mountain of life, it's important to remember that

you should enjoy it and if you don't, then change it.

67)   Kindness in words creates confidence, kindness in thinking creates profoundness, and kindness in giving creates love.
-Lao Tzu

68)   Misery doesn't only love company, it demands it.

69)   The helping hand you're looking for can be found at the end of your arm.

70)   Hope springs eternal.

71)   The strongest memory is paler than the weakest ink.

72)   The shortest distance between two points may be a straight semi-circle.

73)   It is not who is right, but what is right, that is of importance.

74)   People who are successful do things they don't like to do.
-Cynde Denson

75)   It is easier to give the medicine than to take it.
-Uncle Bidz/Tommy Palmer

76)   Love—a fruit that is always in season.
-Mother Theresa

77)   Bacon and eggs — the pig is committed; the chicken is just involved.
—*John Zaleski*

78)   The job is never finished, we just run out of time.
—*Jim Brown*

79)   We are all teachers and all students.

80)   Happiness is a perfume that you cannot pour on others without getting a few drops on yourself.
—*Louis Mann*

81)   Beauty has many dimensions.

82)   Calmness is trust in action.
—*A.A. John Moser*

83)   There is a snarl on every corner on this highway of life.
—*Louie DeLallo*

84)   Take care of the minutes and the hours take care of themselves.

85)   The easy way to become an expert is just to read one book on the subject.
—*Paul Miller*

86)   Tact is the art of convincing people that they know more than you do.

87)   The trouble with doing something right the first time is that nobody appreciates how difficult it was.

88)   The squeaky wheel doesn't always get the grease; sometimes it gets replaced.

89)   In matters of principle, stand like a rock; in matters of taste, swim with the current.

90)   Everything works; it's just a matter of degrees.
         -Ted B.

91)   "If" is not found in the dictionary of life.

92)   Do unto others before they do unto you.

93)   As long as you learn well it doesn't matter how long it takes you.
         —P.J. Land

94)   If a husband and wife get along in the bedroom it's because they get along in other rooms.

95)   Failure is failing to try.

96)   Even a train stops.

97)   It's a strange world of language in which skating on thin ice can get you into hot water.

98)   Action cures fear.
         —John Zaleski

99)   Worry is like a rocking chair—it gets you nowhere.

100)   Always behave like a duck. Keep calm and unruffled on the surface, but paddle like the devil underneath.

101)   We the willing are led by the incompetent leading the unwilling.

102)   There are two kinds of men who never amount to much: those who cannot do what they are told and those who can do nothing else.

103)   It is not always the coldest woman who gets the fur coat.

104)   Silence is the hardest argument to refute.

105)   Never throw mud. You may miss your mark and you'll get your hands dirty.

106)   Managers are people who do things right; leaders are people who do the right things.

107)   If you can't live with the thorns, you won't be able to smell the roses.

108)   To know and not to do is really not to know.

109)   There is an old saying that a man is a fool who can't be angry, but a man is wise who won't be angry.

110)   The worst crime of all is to do well that which shouldn't be done at all.

111)   The world hates change yet it is the only thing that has brought progress.

112)   Originality is the art of concealing your source.

113)   Eighty percent of success is showing up.

114)   The mind is like the stomach; it is not how much you put in it that counts, but how it digests.

115)   Some men are like pyramids that are very broad when they touch the ground but grow narrow as they reach the sky.

116)   The happiest miser on earth is the man who saves up every friend he can make.

117)   The safest way to double your money is to fold it up and put it in your pocket.

118)   Turning the other cheek is a kind of moral jiu-jitsu.

119)   An optimist sees an opportunity in every calamity. A pessimist sees a calamity in every opportunity.

120)   Success is a public affair. Failure is a private matter.

121)   It's better to do something imperfectly than to do nothing perfectly.

122)   Companies don't make purchases; they establish relationships.

123)   At the top there is quality, not quantity.

124)   You can't relieve an itch by stroking it gently.

125)   One computer can do the work of 100 ordinary men but no computer can do the work of one extraordinary man.

126)   Probably the biggest advantage of success is that you don't have to listen to good advice.

127)   Computers are the appliances to the network.

128)   Many things must be done well to succeed but only one thing must be done poorly to fail.

129)   Almost anything you will do will be insignificant but it's very important that you do it.

130)   Happiness is doing with a smile what you have to do anyway.

131)   You show what you know; you sell what you show.

132)   To wonder is to begin to understand.

133)   When in doubt, risk it.

134)   Imagination lit every lamp in this country.

135)   The wise man knows everything; the shrewd man knows everyone.

136)   It's your attitude, not your aptitude, which determines your altitude in life.

137)   Some people are like wheelbarrows—not useful unless pushed, and easily upset.

138)   The greatest use of one's life is to spend it on something that will outlast it.

139)   I still believe in tomorrow.

140)   If you don't understand my silence you will not understand my words.

141)   What I do today is important because I am exchanging a day of my life for it.

142)   It's useless to put your best foot forward and then drag the other.

143)   There is no general rule without some exception.

144)   Things done cannot be undone.

145)   When one door shuts another opens.

146)   Time loses sales.

147)   Revenge is a kind of wild justice.

148)   Give us the tools and we will finish the job.

149)   It is better to wear out than rust out.

150)   Life is made up of marble and mud.

151)   Anger is a short madness.

152)   Let us never negotiate out of fear, but let us never fear to negotiate.

153)   Think like a man of action, act like a man of thought.

154)   An ambassador is an honest man, sent abroad to lie for his country.

155)   How long? As long as it takes to catch a fish.

156)   If the dog hadn't stopped he would have caught the cat.

157)   Even a blind squirrel finds an acorn.

158)   If all economists were laid end to end they would not reach a conclusion.

159)   A great fortune is great slavery.

160)   A man surprised is half beaten.

161)   A wild duck never laid a tame egg.

162)   A wise man changes his mind. A fool never will.

163)   All promises are either kept or broken.

164)   An hour in the morning is worth two in the evening.

165)   He who lies down with dogs will rise with fleas.

166)   He who pays the piper may call the tune.

167)   He who commences many things finishes but few.

168)   Hope for the best and prepare for the worst.

169)   If you kill one flea in March you kill one hundred.

170)   If you want a thing done, go; if not, send.

171)   It is more pain to do nothing than something.

172)   It is not all butter that a cow yields.

173)   Good judgment comes from experience.

174)   Experience comes from poor judgment.

175)   Necessity knows no law.

176)   One beats the bush and another catches the birds.

177)   The busiest men have the most leisure.

178)   The rotten apple injures its neighbors.

179)   There are no easy answers, only intelligent choices.

180)   The hardest problem to resolve is the one you do not know you have.

181)   When you throw dirt you only lose ground.

182)   I have found the enemy; it is I.

183)   Luck is the ability to appreciate an opportunity.

184)   If you are doing what you want to do there is no such thing as not enough time.

185)   Wasting your own time is foolish; wasting somebody else's time is criminal.

186)   The sight of the gallows focuses your attention on the problem.

187)   When life gives you lemons, make lemonade.

188)   It is usually the person in the wrong who becomes angry first.

189)   Thaumaturgy—the performance of miracles.

190)   It is not the employer who pays the wages—he only handles the money.

191)   Never try to push a river.
         —George Downing

192)   A good deed is never cost.

193)   The most powerful weapon on earth is a human soul on fire.

194)   Success is often just an idea away.

195)   Never insult an alligator until after you have crossed the river.

196)   The young man knows the rules but the old man knows the exceptions.

197)   Kindness is a language the deaf can hear and the blind can read.

198)   The greatest man in history was the poorest.

199)   Any man can captain in a calm sea.
        -Kevin Antisdale

200)   Only a lie that is not ashamed of itself can succeed.

201)   I hear and I forget. I see and I remember. I do and I understand.
        -T. Doyle Perry

202)   It's not difficult to be smart—just think of something stupid and do the opposite.

203)   It is the loose ends with which men hang themselves.

204)   Tough times never last but tough people do.
        —Joe Surber

205)   In a jungle you can hack your way; in a swamp, with every step you sink.

206)   You don't make an omelet without breaking eggs.

207)   The man who does only what is required of him is a slave. The moment he does more he's a free man.

208)   If an excuse is good enough, we call it a reason.

209)   To handle yourself, use your head; to handle others, use your heart.

210) It is twice as hard to crush a half-truth as a whole lie.

211) Success is, an amazing amount of time, a positive manipulation of failure.

212) Peace comes not from the absence of conflict in life but from the ability to cope with it.

213) For every vision there are many revisions.
—*Jim Reilly*

214) Inside every large problem is a small problem struggling to get out.

215) Even if you're on the right track, you'll get run over if you just sit there.

216) Love looks through a telescope; envy looks through a microscope.

217) Never try to make anyone like yourself. You know, and God knows, that one of you is enough.

218) Dig a well before you are thirsty.

219) The creation of a thousand forests is in one acorn.

220) Diplomacy is the art of telling someone to go to hell in such a way that he looks forward to making the trip.

221) Behind every successful man is a surprised mother-in-law.

222)   Three important parts of a speech—A: a strong opening, B: a powerful close, and C: the shortest time between A and B.

223)   An outstanding salesman doesn't make sales; he makes customers.

224)   I am only an average man but I work harder at it than the average man.
       -Theodore Roosevelt

225)   Everyone thinks of changing the world but no one thinks of changing himself.
       —Leo Tolstoy

226)   Unfortunately, answers that sound good aren't necessarily good, sound answers.

227)   A good lie finds more believers than a bad truth.
       —German proverb

228)   The trouble with experience is that it usually teaches you something you really didn't want to know.

229)   Revisit your decision.
       —Herman Schuler

230)   Lose an hour in the morning and you'll spend all day looking for it.

231)   You can see a lot by just looking.
       —Yogi Berra

232)   Empathy is the greatest serving you can request.

233)   A camel is a horse designed by a committee.

234)   No product is as good as its service.

235)   Trying to squash a rumor is like trying to unring a bell.

236)   If you're feeling good, don't worry; you'll get over it.

237)   Fortune favors the brave.

238)   Confusion is a local view of things working out in general.

239)   Nothing keeps a man's feet on the ground like having a little responsibility placed on his shoulders.

240)   Failures are divided into two classes—those who thought and never did, and those who did and never thought.

241)   Coming together is a beginning, keeping together is progress, and working together is success.

242)   Success—if you have tried something and failed you are vastly better off than if you tried to do nothing and succeeded.

243)   Failure to plan is planning for failure.

244)   The road to hell is paved with good intentions and roofed with lost opportunities.

245)   The morning is wiser than the evening.
        —*Russian proverb*

246)   The cleverest of lies lasts only a week.
        -Japanese proverb

247)   An after dinner speaker has been defined as the man who talks in other people's sleep.

248)   Good order is the foundation of all good things.

249)   An accordionist, it has been said, is the only one who can successfully play both ends against the middle.
        -Rockefeller/ 16thcentury English proverb

250)   All the strings come up to the puppeteer.

251)   Curiosity is the wick in the candle of learning.

252)   The next best thing to knowing something is knowing where to find it.

253)   The more obligations we accept that are self-imposed, the freer we are.

254)   An idealist believes the short run doesn't count. A cynic believes the long run doesn't matter. A realist believes that what is done or left undone in the short run determines the long run.

255)   Judge a man by his favorite proverbs.
        -*French proverb*

256)   Justice—truth in action.

257)   He who knows the most believes the least.
        -*Italian proverb*

258)   One lie kills a thousand truths.

259)   You can't jump a canyon in two leaps.

260)   Anybody who isn't pulling his weight is probably
        pushing his luck.

261)   A man begins cutting his wisdom teeth the first
        time he bites off more than he can chew.

262)   Self-discipline is when your conscience tells you to
        do something and you don't talk back.

263)   Experience with the past is the crystal ball of the
        future.

264)   Your talents are like floodlights; open them and let
        them shine forth.

265)   No gift is more precious than good advice.

266)   To hold water, use a cup; to hold love, use your
        heart.

267)   Murphy's Law—If you hit two keys on a typewriter,
        the one you don't want hits the paper.

268)   Murphy's 10th Corollary—Mother Nature is a witch.

269)   History doesn't repeat itself. Historians merely repeat themselves.

270)   Murphy's Corollary—No matter how much you do, you'll never do enough.

271)   Young's Law—All great discoveries are made by mistake.

272)   Suicide is the sincerest form of self-criticism.

273)   Kramer's Law—Whenever someone says he's being perfectly frank, he's being less than perfectly frank.

274)   When your work speaks for itself, don't interrupt.

275)   Good health is your best wealth.

276)   One can never consent to creep when one feels an impulse to soar.
       —*Helen Keller*

277)   He that cannot obey cannot command.
       —*Benjamin Franklin*

278)   Everyone lives by selling something.

279)   The trouble with most of us is that we would rather be ruined by praise than saved by criticism.

280)   Brains are like hearts; they go where they are appreciated.
        -*Robert McNamara*

281)   Rudeness is a little person's imitation of power.

282)   Just because a path is well beaten is no proof it's the right one.

283)   The difficult we handle immediately; the impossible takes a while longer.

284)   The more you fail the more you'll succeed.

285)   Manners make the man.

286)   You can't turn the clock back but you can wind it up.

287)   If my mind can conceive it and my heart believe it then I can achieve it.

288)   The work will teach you how to do it.
        —*Estonian proverb*

289)   Man works from sun to sun but a woman's work is never done.

290)   He who has imagination without learning has wings but no feet.

291)   Who shaves the barber?

292)   The man who does all the talking is at a disadvantage.

293)   It's like getting bitten to death live by a duck.

294)   HoJo vanilla is but one of 28 flavors.

295)   Every male body has two heads.
        —*John Izzo*

296)   The one who does the least work will get the most credit.

297)   A house built on Jell-O will not stand.

298)   It's like trying to dent a steel ball bearing with a rubber hammer.

299)   You can screw up a steel ball with a rubber hammer.

300)   Shouting is the mark of a limited mind's inability to express itself.

301)   You have to bleed a little to appreciate a Band-Aid.

302)   Fifty percent of the people know what to say but can't say it. The other fifty percent don't know what to say but keep saying it.

303)   The person doing all the talking is at a disadvantage.

304)   The tugboat pulls the big ship.

305)   Empty barrels make the loudest noise.

306)   Don't dig a hole for somebody else because you might fall in it yourself.

307)   You can spit on a stone but you can't make it wet.

308)   No tree grows to heaven.

309)   No matter how high a person sits he is still sitting on his ass.

310)   How many salesmen do you have? About half.

311)   Many roads lead to the top of a mountain. Don't neglect a new road just because it's new.

312)   It's like eating soup with a fork.

313)   It's better to have your enemies inside your tent pissing out than have them outside the tent pissing in.

314)   The 20-80-20 Rule: Twenty percent of the people do eighty percent of the work, while another twenty percent try to stop what the first twenty percent are doing.

315)   Never expect anything from a woman; you'll never be disappointed.

316)   The hard way is the easy way.

317)   It's hard to sell bread that does not fit into toasters.

318)   Move a muscle, change a thought.
       —*John Moser*

319)   Sympathy is never wasted on someone else; it is only wasted when you give it to yourself.

320)   Yesterday is a canceled check and tomorrow is a promissory note. Only today is cash in hand.

321)   If you have one foot in tomorrow and one in yesterday you'll fall on your ass today.

322)   Never let yesterday use up today.

323)   Today is tomorrow's yesterday that you worried about the day before.
       -*Faith*

324)   The world is full of willing people; some willing to work and the rest willing to let them.

325)   Opportunities are usually disguised as hard work so most people don't recognize them.

326)   Don't believe everything you hear but always listen carefully.

327)   Wishing and hoping often lead to disappointment.

328)   You must experience failure to appreciate success.

329)   The youth of a man will never die unless he murders it.

330)   The key to will power is "want" power. People who want something bad enough can usually find the will power to achieve it.

331)   Courage is not the absence of fear; it is the mastery of it.

332)   The most important thing a father can do for his children is to be a man.

333)   Don't shoot the mailman.
       —*Marc Luce*

334)   The four bones of every organ: Wishbone—wish someone would do something about it. Jawbone—doing all the talking but nothing else. Knucklebone—knocks everything. Backbone—carries the load.

335)   "Nothing" is a good word.

336)   Don't ask where I got the Jeep. Just drive it.

337)   Courage is fear that has said its prayers.

338)   No matter how thin you slice it, there are always two sides.

339)   If you want to soar with the eagles in the morning you can't hoot with the owls all night.

340)   There is no failure except in no longer trying.

341)   The paralysis of analysis.

342)   We sometimes see more clearly when our eyes are closed.

343)   Failure doesn't count unless it's the last time you're going to try.

344)   You never fail until you stop trying.

345)   We are all creatures of habit—some good, some bad.

346)   The higher up the tree the monkey goes the more you see of his ass.

347)   If you were born to be a lemon, no matter how high you reach you'll never be a peach.

348)   A raggedy ride beats a proud walk.

349)   The greatest kindness that I can offer you is always truth.

350)   Use things; love people.

351)   The only failure is not trying.

352)   God does not ask that you succeed; he asks that you do your best.

353)   Our lives would run more smoothly if second thoughts came first.

354)   Bad men excuse their faults; good men abandon theirs.

355)   Treat a man as he is and he will remain as he is. Treat a man as he ought to be and could be, and he will become as he ought to be and could be.

356)   You can get a lot farther with kindness and a gun than with kindness alone.
—*Al Capone*

357)   The problem with the rat race is even if you win you are still a rat.

358)   ARU—All Roached Up.

359)   After the verb "to love," the verb "to help" is the most beautiful verb in the world.

360)   Imagination is more important than knowledge.

361)   The road to success is always under construction.

362)   Every use of authority diminishes it.

363)   Once you accept an idea it is an idea whose time has come.

364)   You are the only teacher you will ever have.

365)   Once you realize you have given your power away, you can make the decision to take it back.

366)   If you don't like the games people play then make up your own games.

367)   Most of the time we don't communicate, we just take turns talking.

368)   Your interpretation of what you see and hear is just that—your interpretation.

369)   Excuses are lack of faith in your own power.

370)   Ultimately you have no choice but to feel what you are feeling.

371)   Divorces are final long before they go to court.

372)   Whatever you are trying to avoid won't go away until you confront it.

373)   You can have only two things in life—reasons and results—and reasons don't count.

374)   Angry people are those who are most afraid.

375)   There is no right or wrong, only consequences.

376)   Others can stop you temporarily; only you can stop you permanently.

377)   We fear the thing we want most.

378)   You are the only teacher you will ever have.

379)   What you are afraid to do is a clear indicator of the next thing you need to do.

380)   The way to win is to make it OK to lose.

381)   What you can't communicate runs your life.

382)   If you require someone to change, you require that person to lie to you.

383)   People concern themselves with being normal rather than with being natural.

384)   Criticize the performance, not the performer.

385)   If you don't start you will never finish.

386)   Once you accept an idea it's an idea whose time has come.

387)   Ninety-nine percent responsibility doesn't work.

388)   It's easier to say what we believe than to be what we believe.

389)   You can love someone and not like the way they act.

390)   Meet me halfway—you need the exercise.

391)   The best way to escape from a problem is to solve it.

392)   It takes both rain and sunshine to make a rainbow.

393)   Where the heart is willing it will find a thousand ways. Where the heart is unwilling it will find a thousand excuses.

394)   Don't judge a book by its contents.
       —*Kevin Antisdale*

395)   Dolt's Law—Nothing is impossible for the man who doesn't have to do it himself.

396)   God gave us limited wisdom but infinite stupidity.

397)   Failure is a part of success.

398)   It is better to keep one's mouth shut and be thought a fool than to open it and remove all doubt.

399)   There is never genius without a tincture of madness.

400)   There is a time to let things happen and a time to make things happen.

401)   The highest form of integrity is saving your own ass.
       —*Selma Mirman*

402)   There are three kinds of lies—lies, damn lies, and statistics.

403)   All things obey money.

404)   Words are women; deeds are men.

405)   Great thoughts reduced to practice become great arts.

406)   Life is just a game; there are no winners and no losers.
        —R.B.

407)   Wrong can be right when you were wrong about being wrong.

408)   Left can be right when right is wrong.

409)   Man learns from history that man learns nothing from history.
        -Santayana

410)   Machine cannot replace man until it learns to drink.

411)   The ballot is stronger than the bullet.

412)   Genius is one of the many forms of insanity.

413)   But if thought corrupts language, language can also corrupt thought.
        -George Orwell

414)   All things change; nothing perishes.

415) Man is born to live, not to prepare to live.
      -Boris Pasternak, "Dr. Zhivago"

416) Your action speaks so loudly I can't hear what you
      are saying.

417) For an aching mind, words are physicians.

418) Not even God can undo what has been done.

419) There is no wealth but life.

420) Truth for any man is that which makes him a man.

421) Dare to be wrong and dream.
      —Leo Buscaglia

422) When you are through learning you are through.

423) Prostitutes are human sacrifices on the altar of
      monogamy.

424) Pleasure is nothing more than an intermission from
      pain.

425) Assassination is the most extreme form of
      censorship.

426) It is only when we forget all our learning that we
      begin to know.

427) The greater man, the greater courtesy.

428) Freedom is nothing else but a chance to be better.

429) It is human nature to think wisely and act foolishly.

430) Human kind cannot bear very much reality.

431) You can't hold a man down without staying down with him.

432) The best is the enemy of the good.

433) Knowledge shrinks as wisdom grows.

434) Sometimes silence is not golden, just yellow.
     -John Izzo

435) Adam ate the apple and our teeth still ache.
     —Hungarian proverb

436) The sky's no longer the limit.
     —Richard Nixon

437) The weakest link in a chain is the strongest because it can break it.

438) Time is like money; the less of it we have the further we make it go.

439) Not all married women are wives.

440) A thousand words will not leave as deep an impression as one deed.

441)   Worry gives a small thing a big shadow.
       — *Swedish proverb*

442)   Fear is a part of courage.

443)   It's OK to forget: when you have to; when you need
       to; when you want to; and as long as what you don't
       remember won't hurt you.

444)   Doing what you like is freedom; liking what you do
       is happiness.

445)   Some people, like flowers, give pleasure just by
       being.

446)   Remember yesterday, dream about tomorrow, but
       live for today.

447)   Never let yesterday use up today.

448)   Don't bring a ham sandwich to a banquet.

449)   Heaven is homemade, hell is self-made.

450)   May you have warmth in your igloo, oil in your
       lamp, and peace in your heart.
       -Eskimo proverb

451)   Sometimes you have to be silent in order to be
       heard.

452)   All things are difficult before they are easy.

453)   All truths are not to be told.
        —John Moser

454)   An empty sack cannot stand upright.

455)   You don't stop playing because you grow old; you
        grow old because you stop playing.

456)   Beautiful flowers grow out of manure.

457)   Some days you eat the bear; some days the bear eats
        you.

458)   They named a street after you—one-way.

459)   Women are like elephants. They are nice to look at
        but I wouldn't want to own one.

460)   Women are like cars on a cold morning—when you
        need them they won't turn over.

461)   A car is like a whore—you pay to get screwed.

462)   The only one that stands between you and greatness
        is yourself.
        -Paul O'Brien

463)   God hates a coward.

464)   The FUD factor: Fear, Uncertainty, and Doubt.
        —Joe Surber

465)   If you finish all your tasks you didn't have enough to do.

466)   There is no such thing as ever getting there.

467)   Life is far too important to be taken seriously.
       -Phyllis Levy

468)   If you are all wrapped up in yourself you are overdressed.

469)   In spite of the cost of living it's still popular.

470)   The less you talk the more you're listened to.

471)   The degree of success is directly proportional to the degree of risk.

472)   No decision is sometimes the worst decision you can make.
       —C.B.J. + J.W.B.

473)   The hardest job is when you do nothing because you don't know when you're done.
       -J.W. Brown

474)   Are you trying to march to the beat of two drums?

475)   Failure is only the opportunity to more intelligently begin again.
       —Henry Ford

476)   The greatest mistake a man can make is to be afraid of making one.

477)   Honesty is the first chapter in the book of wisdom.

478)   The first step towards getting the things you want out of life is this: decide what you want.
         -Ben Stein

479)   When you reach the end of your rope, tie a knot and hang on.

480)   Plan your work and work your plan.

481)   You can only make a dream become a reality when you are awake.

482)   Even a lion must defend himself against flies.

483)   Man is not a creature of circumstance; circumstances are the creatures of man.

484)   It's better to bend than to break.
         -Scottish proverb

485)   Self-conquest is the greatest victory.
         —Plato

486)   Every dog is entitled to one bite.

487)   Round numbers are always false.
         -Samuel Johnson

488)   None but a mule denies his family.
         -Moroccan proverb

489)   The best things in life aren't things.

490)   When you bet more than you can afford to lose you
        learn the game.
        -Teddy Roosevelt

491)   Five percent of the population thinks; fifteen
        percent think they think, and the rest would rather
        die than think.
        -Silo Theory

492)   Don't confuse brilliance with a bull market.

493)   The only exercise I get is jumping to conclusions.

494)   The greatest loss is not death but what dies inside
        of us while we still live.

495)   Haloha=love.

496)   Stop stalling; start doing.

497)   Procrastination of any decision leads to the
        rationalization of failure.

498)   Life is a do-it-yourself project.

499)   Being poor is a state of mind; being broke is a
        temporary situation.

500)   Never trouble trouble 'til trouble troubles you.

501)   May you live all the days of your life.

502)   Better an ugly face than an ugly mind.

503)   There are some defeats more triumphant than victories.

504)   A proverb is a short sentence based on long experience.

505)   He is strong who conquers others; he who conquers himself is mighty.

506)   Youth is not a time of life. It is a state of mind.

507)   Goodness is the only investment that never fails.

508)   It is easier to be a critic than a playwright.

509)   Advice is like clothes; it doesn't fit everybody.

510)   Success is going from failure to failure with no loss of enthusiasm.
         -Winston Churchill

511)   Nothing is as strong as gentleness and nothing is so gentle as real strength.

512)   Luce's Law—No good deed goes unpunished.

513)   Peer's Law—The solution to the problem changes the problem.

514)   Bucy's Law—Nothing is ever accomplished by a reasonable man.
         -Cheo

515)   Even too much sunshine burns.

516)   Mistakes are lessons of wisdom.

517)   Originality is undetected plagiarism.
         -William Inge

518)   Paul's Law—If a hard way can be found to do something, we will find it.

519)   Pressure makes diamonds.

520)   Beauty is ageless.

521)   A fortune-teller doesn't know his own fortune.
         —Joe Palmer

522)   Honey is sweet but the bee stings.
         —Joe Palmer

523)   A friend to all is a friend to none.
         —Joe Palmer

524)   Even a poor shot hits if he shoots enough.
         —E.N.D.

525)   Sometimes what I see blocks my vision.

526)   It is a long way from the head to the heart.

527)   A fish rots from the head down.

528)   The players coach the coach.
        -Jody Grose

529)   There's Samson in every man and Delilah in every woman.

530)   Some beauty cannot be seen.

531)   There are more wealthy poor people than there are wealthy rich people.

532)   Any fool can know something; the power is in understanding something.
        -Albert Einstein

533)   The third law of thermodynamics is that chaos will win.

534)   None of the secrets of success will work unless you do.

535)   Every knock is a boost.

536)   The point is that there is no point.

537)   Intelligent men have a right to disagree.

538)   The color of truth is gray.

539)   The rising tide lifts all boats.
        —John Moser

540)   Everything that has a beginning has an end.

541)   Everything that starts, ends.

542)   Take care of the tree and the fruit will come.

543)   A journey of a thousand miles starts with a single step.

544)   The wise man learns from others' mistakes; the fool learns from his own.
         —*Joe Palmer*

545)   Love needs no teacher.
         —*Joe Palmer*

546)   If one believes everything in books, better no books.
         —*J.A.*

547)   Some are wise; others are otherwise.

548)   Nothing is dearer to me than myself.
         —*Joe Palmer*

549)   Failure is the source of success.
         —*Joe Palmer*

550)   Take profit from a loss.
         —*Joe Palmer*

551)   Nothing is more expensive than a false start.
         —*J.A.*

552)   Sometimes the fastest way to get to an eastern destination is to take a western route.

553)   Make your life a mission, not an intermission.

554)   Our names are labels, plainly printed on the essence of our past behavior.

555)   One must judge men not by their opinions but by what their opinions have made of them.

556)   To measure the man, measure his heart.

557)   If you fill the part it matters not if you like it.

558)   There's no way to move without making waves.
        —*John Moser*

559)   If you have a job without any aggravations you don't have a job.

560)   The undriven don't get there.

561)   Diamond—a bit of carbon that never quit improving itself.

562)   It is a long way from the head to the heart.

563)   Sometimes what I see blocks my vision.

564)   While it's true that there are always two sides there is also the middle.

565)   You can't give what you haven't got.

566)   There are no good guys and no bad guys.

567)   Ignorance is the father of wisdom.

568)   Youth prays for time to pass, only to change when they grow old.

569)   What you say and how you say it determines your future.
       —*Susan Roetter*

570)   The willow demonstrates that there is strength in weakness.

571)   The toughest battle to fight is the battle within.

572)   Everything is done in an instant.

573)   Nothing is so strong as gentleness. Nothing is so gentle as real strength.

574)   Every weed is a flower to someone else.

575)   When you butt heads you end up with a headache.

576)   Data rich; information poor.

577)   He's abnormally normal.

578)   Sometimes you can see more clearly with the heart than with the eyes in your head.

579)   I have the answer—sometimes it's not appropriate to get the answer.

580)   Don't postpone joy.

581)   I understand that it is all right not to understand.

582)   He keeps the plum and gives me the pit.

583)   There's nothing to lose.

584)   Hard work is the yeast that makes the dough rise.
       —*Uncle Bidz Palmer*

585)   It's like speaking Latin to the Greeks.

586)   The man who removed the mountain began by carrying away small stones.
       -*Proverb*

587)   Nobody starts off with a clean slate.

588)   Do you see the light in others or do you see their lampshade?

589)   How we see life is a matter of choice.

590)   The journey down the mountain may be more difficult than the journey up the mountain.

591)   SNAFU—Situation Normal—All Fouled Up.
       —*World War II saying*

592)   It's the incompetent leading the unwilling.
        —*Bill Sulcius*

593)   Time is the physician's assistant.

594)   You will see when you want to look.

595)   Rust is love's first cousin.

596)   In the world of give and take only a few give what it takes.

597)   Remember that when you point a finger at someone you point three back at you.
        -*Don Hanson*

598)   Half of the world's problems are due to poor communications; the other half are due to good communications.

599)   A sturdy oak is just an acorn that stood its ground.

600)   The quality of a person's life is in direct proportion to his commitment to excellence.

601)   When the sun always shines there is a desert below.

602)   Before you can have an intelligent conversation with someone you must first have one with yourself.

603)   Love is not blind.

604)   Don't put off until tomorrow what you can do today, because you may not see a tomorrow.

605)   The good thing about being backed up against a wall is that the only way you can go is forward.

606)   There is only one version of the truth.
         —*Herman Schuler*

607)   A kiss is nature's way of getting two people so close together that they can't see each other's flaws.

608)   People make a plan work; plans alone seldom make people work.
         -*Don Hanson*

609)   Money is a poor master but an excellent servant.
         -*P.T. Barnum*

610)   Don't look for the open door; open your own doors.

611)   What you say interests people, and who you are inspires them.

612)   To think too long about doing a thing often becomes its undoing.

613)   There is no greater loan than a sympathetic ear.

614)   One is many and many are one.

615)   If you find a path with no obstacles it probably doesn't lead anywhere.

616)   Some people live dying; others die living.

617)   Genius does what it must and talent does what it can.

618)   The boy is the father of the man.

619)   Everything is possible in conversation.
        -Amber Gale

620)   The unspoken word is your slave and the spoken word is your master.

621)   What does not come from the heart does not reach the heart.

622)   Are you possessed by your possessions?
        —P.J. Land

623)   Who de-roaches the roach?

624)   It is not only what we do, but also what we do not do, for which we are accountable.

625)   Are you screwdriver inclined?

626)   The lie harms; the truth heals.

627)   He who has a partner has a master.

628)   I like myself the way I am.
       —*Frank Palmieri*

629)   You don't break laws; they break you.

630)   It's easy to stay what you are and tough to become
       what you're not.

631)   Don't do what I do; see what I see.

632)   Important things are important only when they are
       important.
       -*Frank Martinez*

633)   It's important to do the important things that have
       importance.
       —*Frank Martinez*

634)   It's nice to be important but it's more important to
       be nice.

635)   May the words I have to say today be sweet enough
       in case I have to eat them tomorrow.

636)   A repeat customer is very special.

637)   A generous action is its own reward.

638)   In order to get to the rainbow you must deal with
       the rain.
       -*Dolly Parton*

639)   A man needs to concentrate on the problem, not the task.
        —*Thorson Cheyne*

640)   Are you working hard not doing what you're not doing?

641)   When you "bury the hatchet," don't leave the handle sticking out.

642)   Don't wait for something to turn up. Get a spade and dig for it.

643)   Life is like a ladder; every step we take is either up or down.

644)   Most people major on minor things.
        -*Anthony Robbins*

645)   Repetition is the mother of skill.

646)   There is a difference between good, sound answers and answers that sound good.

647)   Dying for your loved ones can be a great act. Living for them can be an even greater act.

648)   Purpose is stronger than outcome.
        -*Anthony Robbins*

649)   When you make a mistake, don't get down on yourself. Remember that doing the right thing wrong is better than doing the wrong thing right.

650)   He who is patient, obtains.
        -Persian proverb

651)   He who works with his hands is a laborer. He who
        works with his hands and his head is a craftsman.
        He who works with his hand, head, and heart is an
        artist. He who works with his hand, head, heart,
        and feet is a salesman. Amen.

652)   The road to someday leads to a town called
        nowhere.

653)   Trust in God and tie up your camels.

654)   Average: the poorest of the best and the best of the
        poorest.

655)   When the game is over the king and pawn go in the
        same box.
        -Italian proverb

656)   Emotion clouds facts.
        —John Zaleski

657)   Imagination is greater than knowledge.
        -Albert Einstein

658)   The rooster may crow but the hen delivers the
        goods.

659)   Good to begin well; better to end well.

660)   The length of service is not as important as the breadth of service.

661)   Setbacks pave the way for comebacks.

662)   Never fear shadows; they just mean that there is light shining somewhere.

663)   Those who hug illusions seldom embrace opportunities.

664)   Opportunity is often missed because we are broadcasting when we should be tuning in.

665)   If you have trouble sleeping, don't count sheep. Talk to the shepherd.

666)   I asked for a sandwich and was given a slice of bread.
       —*John Zaleski*

667)   Wonder is the daughter of ignorance.
       -*16*th-*century proverb*

668)   Hardships color all of life, but you choose the color—color it bright.

669)   Men do not fail—they give up trying.

670)   Think all you speak, but not all you think.

671)   Nothing improves hearing more than praise.

672)   Each day should be unwrapped like a precious gift.

673)   Knowledge finds the path. Wisdom lights it.

674)   When one is out of touch with himself, one cannot touch others.

675)   Honesty is the first chapter in the book of wisdom.
-Thomas Jefferson

676)   You must crack the nuts before you can eat the kernel.

677)   Tact is like a girdle; it enables you to organize the awkward truth more attractively.

678)   Talk is cheap because supply exceeds demand.

679)   First the man takes a drink, then the drink takes a drink, and then the drink takes the man.
-Japanese proverb/John Moser

680)   If you want to gather honey, don't kick over the beehive.

681)   God, make my life not a stumbling block but a stepping-stone for others.

682)   There is a time to let things happen and a time to make things happen.

683) A tongue three inches long can kill a man six feet
      tall.
      -Japanese proverb

684) Add one small bit to the truth and you inevitably
      subtract from it.

685) Confidence is the feeling you sometimes have
      before you fully understand the situation.

686) Houses are visible but homes are not.

687) You can't change the past, but you can ruin a
      perfectly good present by dwelling on the past.

688) Life isn't a race; it's a journey.

689) Three cases where supply exceeds demand are
      taxes, trouble, and advice.

690) Most things worthwhile are often hard to do.
      —John Zaleski

691) The door of success swings on the hinges of
      obstacles.

692) He who has health has hope; and he who has hope
      has everything.
      -Arabian proverb

693) When the student is ready the teacher will appear.
      —Harry Payne

694)   Athletes work hard to create the chance of winning. Champions work even harder to eliminate the chance of losing.
-Mike J. O'Hara

695)   Don't wait for your ship to come in if you have not sent one out.

696)   The highest form of ignorance is to reject something you know nothing about.

697)   If you want to think one year ahead, sow a seed; if you want to think ten years ahead, plant a tree. If you think one hundred years ahead, educate the people.

698)   Emotion is created by motion.

699)   To err is human; to forgive, divine; to forget, foolhardy.

700)   Never mistake knowledge for wisdom. One helps you make a living. The other helps you make a life.
-Sandra Carey

701)   Throughout history the most common debilitating human ailment has been cold feet.

702)   It's not true that nice guys finish last. Nice guys are winners before the game starts.
-Addison Walker

703)   Friends are flowers in the garden of life.

704)   The fewer the facts, the stronger the opinion.

705)   The ancestor of every action is your thought.
        -Wayne Dyer

706)   The first duty of love is to listen.

707)   Birth and death are but two rungs on the ladder of
        life.

708)   In order to profit from your mistakes you must go
        out and make some.

709)   The only complete mistake is the mistake from
        which we learn nothing.

710)   Failure teaches success.

711)   Ideas are cheap.
        —Vladimir Slep

712)   A little extra effort makes the difference between
        mediocrity and greatness.

713)   Efficiency is doing things right; effectiveness is
        doing the right things.

714)   To change your life, change your conversation.

715)   It's better to die on your feet than to live on your
        knees.

716)   Learn to listen—listen to learn.

717)   You cannot think your way into right action; you must act your way into right thinking.

718)   Better a diamond with a flaw than a pebble without.
         -Confucius

719)   Don't count time; make time count.

720)   When it comes to giving, some people stop at nothing.

721)   A man who has committed a mistake and doesn't correct it is committing another mistake.
         —Confucius

722)   If you need a computer and don't buy it, you pay for it, even though you don't have it.
         -Ford/Palmieri

723)   An expert is someone who is called in at the last minute to share the blame.

724)   There is glory in a great mistake.
         -Nathaniel Crane

725)   Every rose has its thorn.

726)   The only real difference between a profit and a loss is that you can spend a profit.

727)   Often we speak loudest in complete silence.

728)   The more the results, the less the conversation.

729)   Success is a decision we make.

730)   Enthusiasm and persistence can make an average person superior; indifference and lethargy can make a superior person average.
        -William A. Ward

731)   If you need a piece of equipment but don't buy it, you pay for it even though you don't have it.
        —Henry Ford

732)   I grow impatient waiting patiently.

733)   Behind an able man there are always other able men.
        —Chinese proverb

734)   Thinking provides thoughts; action provides results.

735)   We devote a great deal of time worrying about not having enough time.

736)   Make haste slowly.

737)   When nobody around you seems to measure up, it's time to check your yardstick.
        -Bill Lemley

738)   The fellow that does not step on somebody's toes is probably standing still.
        -Franklin P. Jones

739)   Getting things done isn't necessarily the same as doing things.

740)   Love: the hunger for one's presence, and the thirst for one's affection.

741)   We should not concern ourselves with how long we live but with living as we are living.

742)   Is your window of life clear?

743)   Dying is the last thing we do...so do it your way.

744)   The river of life has many twists and turns.

745)   It's not what you say; it's how you phrase it.
        —*Kathleen Palmieri Agid*

746)   I've sharpened my pencil so much that I'm down to the eraser.
        -Tammie Burns

747)   Serving—gain without pain.

748)   One battle that is not over until death is the battle of I.

749)   Night is part of day, but day is not part of night.

750)   Stenderup's Law: The sooner you fall behind the more time you have to catch up.

751) I always loved to work.
      —*Filomeno Palmieri*

752) Organization is the key to success; reorganization is the key to failure.

753) It is through our weakness that we find strength.

754) We are all part of nature.

755) If you need a friend, get a dog.
      -Michael Douglas, "Wall Street"

756) Life is like a candle.

757) Don't complain how the ball bounces after you have dropped it.

758) He who is out the door has already a good part of the journey behind him.
      —*Dutch proverb*

759) One man's disaster is another man's fortune.

760) The Son of God became man to enable men to become the sons of God.
      -C.S. Lewis

761) The bitterness of false promises remains long after the sweetness of low price is forgotten.
      -G. Conti

762) Happiness is a decision.

763) The mind has questions. The heart has answers. The mind does not answer and the heart does not question.

764) Business is a lot like a game of tennis—those who don't serve well end up losing.
      -Doc Anklam

765) Children are like mosquitoes—the moment they stop making noises, you know they're getting into something.

766) Things that count most cannot be counted.

767) Life would be more pleasant if we could forget our troubles as easily as we forget our blessings.
      -Tom Haggai

768) There isn't enough darkness in all of the world to snuff out the light of one little candle.
      —Anonymous

769) It's hard to sell from an empty shelf.
      -A Stamford, Connecticut Volvo salesman

770) Life's lessons are tough.
      —Tammie Burns

771) Ability is a good thing but stability is even better.

772) Abilities are like tax deductions—we use them or we lose them.

773)   It is better to master one mountain than one thousand foothills.

774)   All mankind is divided into three classes—those that are immovable, those that are movable, and those that move.
-*Ben Franklin*

775)   None are so old as those who have outlived enthusiasm.

776)   Life is what happens while you're making other plans.

777)   Performance is always better than explanation.

778)   No good deed will go unpunished.

779)   I feel like a team player as a ball kicked around.

780)   Two thousand years ago the Romans said, "Scientia protestas est"—Knowledge is power.

781)   The ability to withstand adversity is the hallmark of greatness.

782)   Swak—soft and gutless; Germorse—a 22-carat screw up.
-*Ron Bainbridge; Unisys, South Africa*

783)   Expert—A man who has a hundred different ways to make love but doesn't know any girls.

784)   The entire ocean is affected by a pebble.

785)   Wisdom is not attained with years but by ability.

786)   The smallest good deed is better than the largest good intention.

787)   There is very little future in being right when your boss is wrong.

788)   The spoken word is your commander; the unspoken is yours to command.

789)   It's like being on a desert island with no compass.

790)   Peter's Prognosis—Spend sufficient time in confirming the need and the need will disappear.

791)   Futility Factor—No experience is ever a complete failure. It can always serve as a negative factor.

792)   Paul's law- you can't fall off the floor.

793)   In crises that force people to choose among alternative courses of action, most people will choose the worst possible one.

794)   Simon's Law—Everything put together falls apart sooner or later.

795)   Katz's Law—Men and nations will act rationally when all other possibilities have been exhausted.

796)   Clark's Second Law—The only way to discover the limits of the possible is to go beyond them into the impossible.

797)   Stewart's Law of Retraction—It is easier to get forgiveness than permission.

798)   Lieberman's Law—Everybody lies but it doesn't matter since nobody listens.

799)   Lynch's Law—When the going gets tough, everyone leaves.

800)   I am a slow walker but I never walk backwards.

801)   A beautiful theory killed by a nasty, ugly little fact.

802)   Carl does the work of two men—Laurel and Hardy.

803)   Tell the truth and run, you go slowly.
       -Proverb

804)   Get your facts first and then you can distort them as much as you please.

805)   Facts do not cease to exist because they are ignored.

806)   The wishbone will never replace the backbone.

807)   Never complain about getting old; many people never get a chance.

808)   The greatest crime a company can commit is to not make a profit.

809)   Learning is a permanent change in behavior.

810)   The only thing worse than death is defeat.

811)   Cows may come and cows may go but the bull in this place goes on forever.

812)   If you will not listen you will never hear.

813)   You can't have a baby in a month by making nine women pregnant.

814)   Success is fathered by many; failure is an orphan.

815)   Time is a man-made concept.

816)   People who wait until they feel like doing a job rarely do.

817)   One worthwhile task carried to a successful conclusion is worth half a hundred unfinished tasks.

818)   If you can give your son only one gift, let it be enthusiasm.

819)   Give a man a fish and he'll eat for a day; teach him how to fish and he will eat for the rest of his life.

820)   One of life's greatest pleasures—paying the last installment.

821)   All proverbs are old; a saying must stand the test of time to become a proverb.

822)   Four things that never return—a spoken word, a sped arrow, the past, and a lost opportunity.
         -Jim Reilly

823)   If at first you don't succeed, try again. Then give up and don't make a fool of yourself.
         -W. C. Fields

824)   Happiness is often a rebound from hard work.

825)   Two dangers constantly threaten the world—order and disorder.

826)   Money is like muck—not good unless it be spread.

827)   Never try to teach a pig to sing; it wastes your time and annoys the pig.

828)   Footprints in the sand are never made sitting down.

829)   Success usually comes to those who are too busy to look for it.

830)   I not only use all the brains I have but all I can borrow.

831)   Business is like riding a bike; either you keep moving ahead or you fall down.

832)   A man can fail many times but he isn't a failure until he gives up.

833)   The system—you can try to fight it, change it, beat it, knuckle under to it, or improve it. But you first have to learn it.

834)   For every ounce of perfume there are six tons of shit.

835)   The higher you go the more dependent you become on others.

836)   Rewards are anti-climactic; the fun is in the doing.

837)   Enthusiasm without knowledge is like running in the dark.

838)   Discipline is the refining fire by which talent becomes ability.

839)   Activity is the road to knowledge.

840)   Diplomacy is the art of letting someone else have your way.

841)   Information is the lifeblood of a business; communication is the circulatory system.

842)   The highest reward for man's toil is not what he gets for it but what he becomes by it.

843)   Beware of half-truths; you may have gotten hold of the wrong half.

844)   When two people agree on everything one of them is doing all the thinking.

845)   Be realistic. Demand the impossible.

846)   That which is used, develops; that which is not used wastes away.

847)   Every man has a right to his opinion, but no man has a right to be wrong in his facts.

848)   Be kind. Remember, everyone you meet is fighting a hard battle.

849)   Attitudes are more important than facts.

850)   When people share their fears with you, share your courage with them.

851)   Giving up is the ultimate tragedy.

852)   Patience: A minor form of despair disguised as virtue.

853)   Wishing without work is like fishing without bait.

854)   You can't build a reputation on what you are going to do.

855)   One never finds life worth living; one always has to make it worth living.

856)   Men do less than they ought unless they do all they can.

857)   There are more goods bought by the heart than by the head.

858)   The happiest people aren't without worries; they have learned to cope with them.

859)   Save gas; fart in a jar.
        —*Joe X.*

860)   "Impossible" is a word to be found only in the dictionary of fools.
        -Napoleon

861)   A good idea that is not shared with others will gradually fade away and bear no fruit, but when it is shared it lives forever because it is passed on from one person to another and grows as it goes.

862)   No one is as tired as a person who does nothing.

863)   The future is the past returning through another gate.

864)   Eschew obfuscation.

865)   He has a lot of class; it's all third.

866)   If you don't try you can't fail.

867)   A seven-course Irish dinner—a six-pack and a potato.
       —*Joe Surber*

868)   Enthusiasm without knowledge is hysteria.

869)   Organization is the key to success.

870)   Don't let yesterday use up today.

871)   Experience is what you get when you were expecting something else.

872)   There's nothing like a little experience to upset a theory.

873)   Good supervision is the art of getting average people to do superior work.

874)   A fault recognized is half corrected.

875)   The joy is in creating, not maintaining.
       -Vince Lombardi

876)   "Anger" is only one letter short of "danger."

877)   To contrive is nothing; to construct is something; to produce is everything.

878)   Knowledge is better than riches.

879)   Spinoza's Law—If facts conflict with a theory either the theory must be changed or the facts.

880)   The great thing about computers is that there are just as many mistakes as ever but now they are nobody's fault.

881)   Idealism increases in direct proportion to one's distance from the problem.

882)   A man wrapped up in himself makes a very small package.

883)   Even the noblest dog should have a few fleas; that way the dog always remembers he is a dog.

884)   Follow up isn't just leaving a message or writing a letter; it's making sure the job gets done.

885)   Correction does much; encouragement does more.

886)   What's worse, the blind leading the blind or the blind talking to the deaf?

887)   Never avoid the opportunity to keep your mouth shut.

888)   Snowflakes are one of nature's most fragile things but just look at what they can do when they stick together.

889)   Temper, if ungoverned, governs the whole man.

890)   Auditors are the people who go in after the war is lost and bayonet the wounded.

891)   Olmstead's Law—After all is said and done a hell of a lot more is said than done.

892)   Woehike's Law—Nothing is done until nothing is done.

893)   Upward mobility rule—Don't be irreplaceable. If you can't be replaced you can't be promoted.

894)   Vaughan's Rule of Corporate Life—The less important you are on the table of organization the more you'll be missed if you don't show up.

895)   What seems so necessary today may not even be desirable tomorrow.

896)   Anything really worthwhile in this life takes time to build.

897)   Nothing chastens planners more than the knowledge that they will have to carry out their plans.

898)   Disillusionment is the first step toward wisdom.

899)   Dude's Law of Duality—Of two possible events, only the undesired one will occur.

900)   Every great achievement once was impossible.

901)   Silence is often mistaken for wisdom.

902)   It's far greater to get a hold of yourself than someone else.

903)   POETIS—Piss On Everything, Tomorrow Is Saturday.

904)   It's not the hours you put in but what you put into each hour that counts.

905)   A lie stands on one foot; truth on two.

906)   Everything new was not standard at one time.

907)   Diplomacy is the art of telling someone to go to hell in such a way that he looks forward to making the trip.

908)   I feel like a mushroom—everyone keeps me in the dark and feeds me shit.

909)   Statistics are like loose women; once you get them down you can do anything you want with them.

910)   Silence is often mistaken for wisdom.

911)   The secret of motivation is hope.

912)   A little daily dose of success is enough to keep most of us going.

913)   One good man is better than three fair ones.

914)   It is impossible to defeat an ignorant man by argument.

915)   The acid test of intelligence is its ability to cope with unintelligence.

916)   Aren't you glad you didn't answer all the knocks of opportunity?

917)   Skepticism is slow suicide.

918)   Accuracy is the twin brother of honesty; inaccuracy of dishonesty.

919)   Heaven never helps the man who will not act.

920)   When a man seeks your advice he generally wants your praise.

921)   The wildest colts make the best horses.

922)   It is great cleverness to know how to conceal one's cleverness.

923)   Success often comes from not knowing your limitations.

924)   Our greatest glory consists not in never losing, but in rising every time we fail.

925)   Never let logic interfere with your thinking.

926)   Business will be better or worse.

927)   We are all manufacturers. Some make good, others make trouble, and still others make excuses.

928)   Never appeal to a man's better nature. He may not have one.

929)   Invoking his self-interest gives you more leverage.

930)   A little learning is a dangerous thing, but a little patronage more so.

931)   Any fool can criticize, condemn, and complain, and most fools do.

932)   To be conscious that you are ignorant of the facts is a great step to knowledge.

933)   The art of statesmanship is to foresee the inevitable and expedite its occurrence.

934)   Men don't plan to fail but fail to plan.

935)   You'll crush your laurels if you rest on them.

936)   You never get a second chance to make a good first impression.

937)   All idealism is falsehood in the face of necessity.

938)   The minority is always wrong—in the beginning.

939)   The superior man understands what is right; the inferior man knows what sells.

940) Always listen to the experts. They'll tell you what can't be done and why. Then do it.

941) To stay young requires unceasing cultivation of the ability to unlearn old falsehoods.

942) You can go wrong by being too skeptical as readily as by being too trusting.

943) An expert is an ordinary person a long way from home.

944) The joy is in creating, not in maintaining.

945) Failure is the path of least persistence.

946) No one is a failure who is enjoying life.

947) Live and let live is fine. But live and help live is better.

948) Sometimes silence makes the best conversation.

949) Age doesn't matter unless you're cheese.

950) Unless the job means more than the pay, it will never pay more.

951) Generous gestures yield the most when that isn't their purpose.

952) The mind boggles and having boggled, moves on.

953)   The wheel always turns.

954)   Harvest while the sun is shining.

955)   Knowledge is a matter of science and no dishonesty or conceit whatsoever is permissible. What is required is definitely the reverse—honesty and modesty.

956)   Habits are strong but brittle and usually break when dropped.

957)   To err is human; to keep people from knowing is divine.

958)   Nothing inoculates the mind against truth as well as ideology.

959)   The best way to avoid being wrong is to admit you do not know the answer.

960)   To wonder is to begin to understand.

961)   I still believe in tomorrow.

962)   Today's success was yesterday's failure that would not give up.

963)   He who controls the information, controls.

964)   If you don't know what you want to do it's harder to do it.

965)   What we anticipate seldom occurs; what we least expect generally happens.

966)   The only sure thing about luck is that it will change.

967)   Material possessions—The more you possess, the more they possess you.

968)   The man who never alters his opinion is like standing water that breeds reptiles of the mind.

969)   One of the rarest things that a man ever does is to do the best he can.

970)   We have a million reasons for failure but not a single excuse.

971)   Nothing is good or bad except by comparison.

972)   Moderation in temper is always a virtue but moderation in principle is always a vise.

973)   Nothing succeeds faster than failure.

974)   Genius is one percent inspiration and ninety-nine percent perspiration.

975)   Society can exist only on the basis that there is some amount of polished lying and that no one says exactly what he means.
       —*Chairman Mao's Little Red Book*

976)   It's an ill wind that blows no good.

977)   A wise man creates more opportunities than he finds.

978)   We never have the time to do the job right the first time but we always have the time to do it a second time.

979)   The dictionary is the only place you will find "success" before "work."

980)   Prejudice is the child of ignorance.

981)   Your greatest fault is to imagine you have none.

982)   The secret to happiness is in liking what one has to do and not doing what one likes to do.

983)   Never be diverted from the truth by what you would like to believe.

984)   If a cluttered desk is a sign of a cluttered mind, what is an empty desk a sign of?

985)   He who laughs last does not get the joke.

986)   The greatest use of one's life is to spend it on something that will outlast it.

987)   To err is human; to forgive, divine.

988) Too much sanity may be madness. The greatest madness of all may be to see life as it is, not as it should be.

989) Often greatness comes veiled in simplicity.

990) Work is the curse of the English drinking class.

991) Do not criticize another man until you have walked a mile in his moccasins.

992) An ounce of determination is worth a ton of procrastination.

993) The best attitude is a "keep-at-it-tude."

994) Some people live to work; others work to live.

995) Every accomplishment great or small starts with the same decision—"I'll try."

996) It's like asking a rabbit to look after your carrots.

997) Constructive criticism is only as good as its usefulness.
—*Howard Berger*

998) The most destructive criticism is indifference.

999) To rest is to rust; to be active is to achieve.

1000) If you do not understand my silence you will not understand my words.

1001)   Wisdom is the ability to discover alternatives.

1002)   Please energize brain before putting mouth in gear.

1003)   Don't confuse effort with progress.

1004)   History repeats itself because we do not learn by our mistakes.

1005)   There are truths that are neither for all men nor for all time.

1006)   The road to hell is paved with good intentions.

1007)   A good memory is a fine thing but so is the ability to forget.

1008)   Ergasiophobia—fear of work. Phronemophobia—fear of thinking.

1009)   Depression is the first step towards feeling better.

1010)   Confucius say top of ladder nice place to be but very lonesome.

1011)   Fear is the parent of cruelty.

1012)   Life is short but truth works far and lives love; let us speak the truth.

1013)   Tell the truth and so confound and puzzle your adversaries.

1014)   A good supervisor is someone who can step on your toes without messing up your shine.

1015)   The only good is knowledge and the only evil is ignorance.
-Socrates

1016)   Man is born to live and not to prepare to live.

1017)   Some minds are like concrete—permanently set and all mixed up.

1018)   Frustration builds some men and breaks others.

1019)   A computer automates the lie.

1020)   Pray for what you want but work for the things you need.

1021)   The difference between business and government is that government has no bottom line.

1022)   Old salesmen never die; they just go out of commission.

1023)   It takes all of the running you can do to stay in the same place. If you want to get somewhere else you must run at least twice as fast.

1024)   Discontent is the first step in the progress of man.

1025)   Dissatisfaction without discouragement breeds progress.

1026)   To get someone's consideration, give him yours.

1027)   One day of bravery is worth one hundred of cowardice.

1028)   Don't jump to conclusions; dig for facts.

1029)   A leader shuns responsibility at his own peril.

1030)   If you keep your eyes on yesterday, the future will be bumpy.

1031)   Life is a game and all you need do is to learn how to play it.
        —*Susan Kellogg*

1032)   It works because Fred and I are friends.
        —*Julie Hartman*

1033)   What you give out returns to you.
        —*Susan Roetter*

1034)   You are greater than you think you are.
        —*Susan Palmieri*

1035)   Do not worry if you are not rewarded in this world; you will be rewarded in the next.
        —*Vinny Palmieri*

1036)   Focus on the good; whatever you think about you will manifest.
        —*Susan Palmieri*

1037) Bring this or something better. Amen.
       —*Susan Palmieri*

1038) Do what you love and the money will follow.
       —*Susan Palmieri*

1039) We are all addicted. We are either addicted to our commitments or we are addicted to our addictions.
       -*A. Justin Sterling*

1040) The mind is a poor place to store things. It gets all mixed up.
       -*Werner Erhard*

1041) Personal power—the ability to take action.
       -*Anthony Robbins*

1042) Find any excuse to get into a 12-step program.
       -*M. Scott Peck*

1043) It's not what you say it's how you say it.
       -*Deborah Tannen*

1044) You can manifest what you want in life.
       -*Florence Scovill Shinn*

1045) You will see it when you believe it.
       -*Wayne Dyer*

1046) In some ways you never really get over divorce, especially if you have children.
       -*Abigail Trafford*

1047)   Smile. People will think you're crazy. Smile anyway.
        -Leo Buscaglia

1048)   I was thrown an anchor when I needed a life raft.
        -Tom Palmer

Thanks to the special everyday contributors to my life:

Kathleen Agid
Kevin Antisdale
Lou Aquavia
Ron Bainbridge
Ted Balbanus
Howard Berger
Jim Brown
Tammie Burns
Walt Capone
Sandra Carey
Yolanda Chevez
Thorson Cheyne
G. Conti
Lou Delallo
Cynde Denson
Mike Douglas
George Downing
Amber Gayle
Faith Genden
Jody Grose
Tom Haggai
Don Hanson
Julie Hartman
John Izzo
Franklin P. Jones
Susan Kellogg
P.J. Land
Bill Lemley
C.S. Lewis
Phyllis Levy

Marc Luce
Lewis Mann
Frank Martinez
Selma Merman
Karen Mileski
Paul Miller
John Moser
Linda Mullin
Flo O'Brien
Paul O'Brien
Michael J. O'Hara
Joe Palmer
Uncle Bidz Palmer
Tom Palmer
Frank Palmieri
Filomeno Palmieri
Vinny Palmieri
Susan Palmieri
Harry Payne
T. Doyle Perry
Jim Reilly
Susan Roetter
Judy Rudnick
Herman Schuler
Vladimir Slep
Bill Sulcius
Joe Surber
John Zaleski

Additional thanks to the following well-known contributors:

Doc Anklam
P.T. Barnum

Yogi Berra
Leo Buscaglia
Al Capone
Confucius
Nathaniel Crane
Wayne Dyer
Ralph Waldo Emerson
W.C. Fields
Henry Ford
Ben Franklin
Willian Inge
Thomas Jefferson
Samuel Johnson
Art Linkletter
Vince Lombardi
Chairman Mao
Michelangelo
Napoleon
Richard Nixon
Dolly Parton
Anthony Robbins
Nelson Rockefeller
Theodore Roosevelt
Ben Stein
Mother Theresa
Leo Tolstoy
Lao Tse
Addison Walker
Woodrow Wilson
Boris Pasternak, "Dr. Zhivago"